Mr. Fin's Trip

Written by Carolyn Clark

Illustrated by George Ulrich

Mr. Fin took a trip on a ship.

Mr. Fin took a trip on a ship.

Mr. Fin took a trip, and he took it on a ship.

Mr. Fin took a trip on a ship.

3

Mr. Fin's new pants didn't fit.

Mr. Fin's new pants didn't fit.

4

He put on a grin, and he pulled
his tummy in.

Mr. Fin's new pants didn't fit.

5

Mr. Fin felt his pants go r-r-r-ip!

Mr. Fin felt his pants go r-r-r-ip!

Mr. Fin went to sit, and he felt his pants go rip.

Mr. Fin felt his pants go r-r-r-ip!

7

Mr. Fin got a big safety pin.

Mr. Fin got a big safety pin.

He said, "I need this pin to keep my tummy in."

Mr. Fin got a big safety pin.